Yo' MAMA IS So...

1,042 Insults, Comebacks, Putdowns & Wisecracks About Yo' Whole Family!

YO' MAMA IS SO...

With Nasty Putdowns of Famous People by Famous People!

HUGH PAYNE

Illustrations by Martha Gradisher

BLACK DOG
& LEVENTHAL
PUBLISHERS
NEW YORK

ISBN-13: 978-1-57912-726-8

Library of Congress Cataloging-in-Publication Data
Payne, Hugh.
  Yo' mama is so— : 1,042 insults, comebacks, putdowns & wisecracks about yo' whole family! / Hugh Payne ; illustrated by Martha Gradisher.
      p. cm.
  ISBN 1-57912-726-6
  1. Family—Humor. 2. Invective. I. Title. II. Title: Your mama is so—.

  PN6231.F3P39 2007
  818'.602—dc22

                                    2006039326

Cover and interior design: Cindy LaBreacht
Illustrations: Martha Gradisher
Manufactured in the United States of America

Published by
Black Dog & Leventhal Publishers, Inc.
151 West 19th Street
New York, New York 10011
www.blackdogandleventhal.com

Distributed by
Workman Publishing Company
225 Varick Street
New York, NY 10014

g f e d c

CONTENTS

PROLOGUE
How to Use This Book 9

CHAPTER ONE
Yo' Mama's So Dumb... 11

CHAPTER TWO
Yo' Mama's So Fat... 67

CHAPTER THREE
Yo' Mama's So Ugly... 115

CHAPTER FOUR
Yo' Mama's So Old... 139

CHAPTER FIVE
Yo' Mama's So Poor... 169

CHAPTER SIX
She's the Worst: A Miscellany of Insults 181

CHAPTER SEVEN
Oh Yeah? Comebacks for Yo' Mama 213

EPILOGUE
I Promise I'll Never Use This Book Again 255

This book is dedicated
to all the little people
I've insulted all my life.

Sorry.

Perhaps this book will,
in some small way,
repay you for bearing the brunt
of all my abuse all those years.
Or not.

Either way, get over it already.

Prologue
HOW TO USE THIS BOOK

**Taking to pieces is the trade
of those who cannot construct.**
—RALPH WALDO EMERSON

Anyone reading this has or had a mama. Let me just set you straight: I've got nothing against yo' mama. Most mamas are sweet, loving people. Some have their problems. I hope yours has a sense of humor.

In this book, I've tried to perform a civil service by assembling a handy collection of wisecracks, putdowns, and insults for all occasions. Whether your target is someone who's fat, ugly, stupid—or whatever—you'll find some good zingers in these pages to set that person straight. True, many of the nastiest insults target dear old mama, but there's also a healthy variety of jabs at father, brother, sister…even you. Keep in mind that these cracks can actually be used interchangeably, whenever you spot somebody who needs to be put in his or her place. I've tried to be an equal-opportunity insulter, so anyone is fair game. And because, deep down, I'm a nice guy, I've provided mama with some snappy comebacks of her own, should she start to feel abused.

Let me leave you with a little friendly advice: Use *Yo' Mama Is So…* with care and with a smile—and if all else fails, RUN. If you end up getting your face slapped or your butt kicked as a result of the material in this book, sorry, pal, not my problem. Exactly how dumb are you, anyway?

chapter one
YO' MAMA'S SO DUMB...

...she put a quarter in a parking meter and waited half an hour for a gum ball.

Yo' mama's so dumb she puts lipstick
on her head just to make up her mind.

Yo' mama's so dumb you need to put a
minus sign before her IQ.

Yo' mama's so dumb that when she
went to the movies and it said
"Under 17 not admitted," she went back
and got 16 of her friends.

I told yo' brother that Christmas
was right around the corner,
so he went looking for it.

Yo' daddy's so dumb he thinks
the Kentucky Derby is a hat.

Yo' sister has a pretty little head.
For a head, it's pretty little.

Yo' daddy researched the family tree
and discovered he was the sap.

You should study to be a bone specialist—
you have the head for it.

You're so stupid you looked in the mirror
and said, "Who's that?"

Yo' daddy was one of the first to get
a brain…before they were perfected.

WOODY ALLEN ON DIANE KEATON
In real life, Keaton believes in God.
But she also believes
that the radio works because
there are tiny people in it.

You're so stupid you sold your car
for gas money.

When they handed out brains,
yo' brother thought they said "trains"
and said he already had a set.

I'm trying to see things from your
point of view, but I can't get my head
that far up my butt!

Your brain waves fall a little short
of the beach.

You're so dumb, when the police said you
broke the speed limit you offered to fix it.

What you lack in intelligence,
you more than make up for in stupidity.

When yo' daddy said it was chilly outside,
yo' mama ran out with a spoon.

You make me believe in reincarnation.
Nobody can be as stupid as you
in one lifetime.

You possess a mind not merely twisted
but actually sprained.

Yo' mama's so stupid she stepped
on a crack and broke her own back.

Yo' mama's so stupid
she thinks Fleetwood Mac is a new
hamburger at McDonald's.

Yo' brother's so stupid he sits on the TV
and watches the couch.

Yo' mama's so stupid that she thought
Boyz II Men was a day-care center.

Yo' mama's so stupid that when saw
a "Wet Floor" sign, she did.

When you were born, yo' mama
looked at your umbilical cord and said,
"Wow, it comes with cable!"

Yo' mama's so stupid she tried to return
a jigsaw puzzle because it was broken.

Yo' mama's so stupid she attempted
suicide by jumping off the curb.

Yo' brother's so stupid I caught him
peeking around a glass wall to see what
was on the other side.

Yo' mama's so stupid she invented
a silent car alarm.

Yo' mama's so stupid she watches
the Three Stooges and takes notes.

W. C. FIELDS ON MAE WEST
A plumber's idea of Cleopatra.

You're so stupid you returned a donut
because it had a hole in it.

Yo' daddy's so stupid he drilled a peephole
through a window.

Ignorance can be cured. Stupid is forever.

If you were twice as smart,
you'd still be stupid.

I'm not as dumb as you look.

Judging by the old saying "What you don't
know can't hurt you," you're invulnerable.

Keep talking, someday you'll say
something intelligent!

Listen, are you always this stupid or are you just making a special effort today?

Don't go to a mind reader; go to a palm reader. I KNOW you've got a palm.

Yo' mama's so stupid she got fired from the M&M factory for throwing away all the W's.

Yo' brother's so dumb he set fire to the house with a CD burner.

Yo' mama's so stupid that on
her job application, under "Education,"
she put "Hooked on Phonics."

When yo' sister asked me
what kind of jeans I wore, I said Guess,
and she said "Uhhh, Levi's?"

Yo' mama's so stupid
she makes Beavis and Butt-Head
look like Nobel Prize winners.

Yo' sister's so stupid
she can't read an audio book.

CHEVY CHASE ON BOB HOPE

Bob Hope is still about as funny as he ever was. I just never thought he was that funny in the first place.

Yo' daddy's so stupid he thought
the Nazis were saying, "Hi, Hitler!"

Yo' sister's so stupid it takes her a day
to cook a 3-minute egg.

Yo' mama's so dumb she asked me,
"What's the letter after X?" When I said
"Y" she said, "'Cause I wanna know"!

At the bottom of the credit card
application where it said "Sign here,"
yo' brother wrote, "Sagittarius."

I bet your brain runs good as new—
seeing as how you've never used it.

I heard you got a brain transplant—
and the brain rejected YOU!

Yo' mama's so stupid
her shoes say TGIF:
Toes Go In Front.

Yo' brother was walking down
the street yelling into an envelope.
He said he was sending a voice mail.

Yo' sister's so dumb she thinks mohair
is the fur of a mo.

Yo' mama's so stupid if you
gave her a penny for her thoughts,
you'd get change.

Yo' mama's so stupid, on her
job application, where it says
"Emergency contacts," she put
"None, I wear glasses."

Yo' mama's so dumb she asked for a price check at the dollar store.

Calling you an idiot would be an insult to retarded people.

Yo' brother's so stupid he called the 7-Eleven to see when they closed.

Yo' daddy couldn't tell which way an elevator was going if I gave him two guesses.

Yo' grandpa's so stupid he died before
the police arrived because he couldn't find
the "11" button to call "911."

Nobody is saying you're dumb.
It's just that you were 16 years old
before you learned to wave bye-bye.

Oh my God!!! What's that big ugly thing
on your neck?! Oh…it's just your head.

Ordinarily people live and learn.
You just live.

People say that you are the perfect idiot.
I say that you are not perfect—
but you're trying.

CLIFF RICHARD ON GEORGE HARRISON

If you see George Harrison,
you can tell him that I think
he's a load of old rope.

I'd ask how old you are,
but I know you can't count that high.

Yo' brother's so stupid he phoned me
to get my number.

Yo' mama's so dumb she holds conversations with her answering machine instead of calling anyone back.

Yo' sister's got a body that won't quit and a brain that won't start.

If brains were rain, you'd be a desert.

If brains were dynamite, you wouldn't have enough to blow your nose.

If brains were gas, you wouldn't have enough to power a scooter around the inside of a Froot Loop.

You're so dumb you think invisible ink
comes out of a Magic Marker.

Yo' mama's so stupid she got hit
by a coffee cup and told the cops
she got mugged.

Brains aren't everything.
In fact, in your case they're nothing!

Yo' sister's so stupid, when you say
"Wait a minute," she starts counting
"One hippopotamus, two
hippopotamus...."

Yo' brother's so dumb he thinks
the Indie 500 is a music festival.

Yo' daddy's so stupid, when he changes the
clocks he falls forward and springs back.

GEORGE HARRISON ON PAUL MCCARTNEY
**I'd join a band with John Lennon
any day, but I wouldn't join
a band with Paul McCartney.**

Yo' mama's so stupid she thinks an express
train takes overnight to arrive.

It's not just that you have diarrhea
of the mouth; you've got constipation
of the brain.

Yo' brother's so stupid he needs a tutor
to learn how to scribble.

BING CROSBY ON ELVIS PRESLEY
He never contributed
a damn thing to music.

Yo' daddy has a mechanical mind.
Too bad he forgot to wind it up
this morning.

ELVIS COSTELLO ON STING

Somebody should clip Sting around the head and tell him to stop singing in that ridiculous Jamaican accent.

You have one brain cell
and it is fighting for dominance.

You always look lost in thought but who
can blame you—it's unfamiliar territory.

Dr. Frankenstein could use yo' brother
as a blueprint to build an idiot.

Yo' mama's so stupid she ordered
her sushi well done.

Yo' mama's so stupid she ran out of gas
pulling out of the Texaco station.

Yo' mama's so stupid I told her I was
reading a book by Homer and she asked
if I had anything written by Bart.

You're so dumb you dialed information
to get the number for the operator.

Yo' mama's so stupid, when she tried
to commit suicide by jumping off a
building, she got lost on the way down.

Yo' daddy's so stupid he'd need twice as
much sense to be a half-wit.

Yo' sister's so stupid she told me
to meet her at the corner of "Walk"
and "Don't Walk."

Yo' mama's so stupid, when the computer
said, "Press any key to continue,"
she couldn't find the "any" key.

Yo' daddy's so stupid he thought Tupac Shakur was a Jewish holiday.

Yo' brother's so stupid, when I was drowning and yelled for a lifesaver, he said, "Cherry or grape?"

LOU REED ON PETE TOWNSHEND

He is so talentless, and as a lyricist he's profoundly untalented and philosophically boring.

Your daddy's so stupid he sent me a fax with a stamp on it.

Yo' mama's so stupid she sold the house
to pay the mortgage.

Yo' daddy's so stupid
he thinks a sanitary belt is drinking
a shot out of a clean glass.

Yo' brother's so stupid he thinks
Christmas wrap is Snoop Dogg's
holiday album.

Yo' mama's so stupid she thinks
Johnny Cash is a pay toilet.

Yo' brother's so stupid he thinks
"socialism" means partying.

Yo' mama's so stupid she thinks Taco Bell
is a Mexican phone company.

Yo' brother's not stupid; he's possessed
by a retarded ghost.

Yo' mama's so stupid she thinks
Tiger Woods is a forest in Africa.

Yo' daddy's so stupid he thinks a lawsuit
is something you wear to court.

Yo' dog is so stupid he couldn't find
a bone in the butcher shop!

Don't let your mind wander—
it's too little to be let out alone.

Yo' mama's so stupid she took the Pepsi
challenge and chose Skippy.

Yo' brother's so stupid he tried to drop
acid but the car battery broke his toe.

Yo' sister's so dumb she tried to do blow
and inflated her head.

Yo' mama's so stupid she tried
to drown a fish.

Yo' mama's so stupid she tried to mail
a letter with food stamps.

Yo' brother's so dumb he thinks
two-way radio is a stereo.

Yo' mama's so stupid she stole
a free sample.

Yo' brother's so stupid he tried to strangle
himself with a cordless phone.

Yo' mama's so stupid
she tried to throw a bird off a cliff.

Yo' brother's so dumb he tried to get high
and glued his nostrils shut.

LOU REED ON FRANK ZAPPA
Frank Zappa couldn't write a decent
song if you gave him a million and
a year on an island in Greece.

Yo' mama's so stupid she tried to wake up

a sleeping bag.

WILL ROGERS ON CALVIN COOLIDGE
Calvin Coolidge didn't say much, and when he did, he didn't say much.

Yo' mama's so stupid she went to an L.A. Clippers game to get a haircut.

Yo' mama's so stupid she went to the Gap to get her teeth fixed.

Yo' mama's so stupid, when she saw the choices under "Sex" on an application she marked wrote in "sometimes Wednesday."

Yo' mama's so stupid she tried to drown herself in a carpool.

Yo' brother's so stupid, when I asked him if he wanted to play one on one, he said, "Okay, but when do we choose up sides?"

When yo' mama heard that 90 percent of all accidents occur at home, she moved.

Yo' daddy's so stupid, when he saw a "Wrong Way" sign in his rearview mirror, he put the car in reverse.

Yo' mama's so stupid,
when she saw the sign "Airport Left,"
she turned around and went home.

Yo' mama's so stupid,
when she went by the YMCA she said,
"Hey, they spelled 'Macy's' wrong."

Yo' daddy's so stupid,
when he missed the 44 bus
he took the 22 twice instead.

Yo' brother's so stupid, when the judge
said, "Order in the court" he said, "I'll have
a cheeseburger and a Coke."

Yo' mama's so stupid she spent twenty minutes lookin' at an orange juice container because it said "concentrate."

Yo' mama's so stupid, when she asked me what "yield" meant, and I said, "Slow down," she said, "What... does...yield...mean?"

Yo' mama is so stupid she took you to rehab because you were hooked on phonics.

Yo' mama's so stupid she thought Delta Airlines was a sorority.

Yo' mama's so dumb she thought a quarterback
was an income tax refund.

Yo' mama's so stupid
she thought Meow Mix was
a dance record for cats.

Yo' mama's so stupid she thought
Velveeta was a kind of fabric.

Yo' daddy's so stupid
he thought Sherlock Holmes
was a housing project.

Yo' mama's so stupid
she thought Thailand was
a men's clothing store.

Yo' brother's so stupid
he told everyone he was "illegitimate"
because he can't read.

Yo' mama's so stupid she took lessons
on a player piano.

Yo' mama's so stupid she put on her
glasses to watch *20/20*.

Yo' mama doesn't hesitate
to speak her mind because
she has nothing to lose.

ABRAHAM LINCOLN ON STEPHEN A. DOUGLAS
His argument is as thin as the
homeopathic soup that was made by
boiling the shadow of a pigeon that had
been starved to death.

The closest you'll ever get to a brainstorm
is a slight drizzle.

They just invented a new coffin
that goes over the head. It's for people
like you: dead from the neck up.

BELLA ABZUG ON GERALD FORD

**Nixon impeached himself.
He gave us Ford as his revenge.**

I can't have a battle of wits with you.
I never pick on an unarmed man.

Too bad stupidity isn't painful.

Whatever anyone says to you goes
in one ear and out the other—
and NOTHING is blocking traffic.

Yo' daddy's so stupid he thinks a satellite dish revolves around the house.

Yo' brother's so stupid he thinks the New Testament was written after the Pilgrims discovered America.

When God made intelligence rain down upon the Earth you were holding an umbrella.

It's uncanny…when I look into your eyes I can see the back of your head.

You say you are always up bright and
early…well, you're HALF right!

Yo' mama's so stupid she climbed
a chain-link fence to see what
was on the other side.

Yo' brother's so stupid he got stabbed
in a shootout.

Yo' mama's so stupid she stopped at a stop
sign, then waited for it to say go.

THOMAS JEFFERSON ON PATRICK HENRY
All tongue, without
either head or heart.

Yo' brother's so stupid,
when he saw a billboard that said
"Dodge Trucks" he jumped
in and out of traffic.

Yo' daddy's so stupid he locked his keys
in the car and it took him all day
to get your family out.

JOHN ADAMS ON GEORGE WASHINGTON

That Washington was not a scholar is certain. That he is too illiterate, unlearned, unread for his station and reputation is equally beyond dispute.

Yo' mama's so stupid she failed a survey.

Yo' mama's so stupid she got locked out of a convertible with the top down.

Yo' brother's so stupid that
when he threw a grenade at me
I had to pull the pin out for him
and throw it back.

Yo' mama's so stupid
she took you to the drive-in to see
"Closed for the Season."

Yo' father's so stupid he stands
on the corner with a sign that says,
"Will eat for food."

Yo' mama's so stupid she got locked
in a furniture store and slept on the floor.

Yo' mama's so stupid she peels M&M's
to make chocolate chip cookies.

Yo' mama's so stupid she uses
Old Spice in all her cooking.

Yo' brother's so stupid he threw a rock
at the ground and missed.

Yo' mama's so stupid if she spoke her
mind, she'd be speechless.

Yo' daddy's so stupid he went
to the store to buy a color TV and asked,
"What colors ya got?"

Yo' brother's so stupid, when the teacher
asked what a pronoun was,
he said it was a noun that gets paid.

Yo' mama's so stupid she failed
her blood test.

Yo' mama's so stupid she thought
Hamburger Helper came with another
person.

Yo' mama's so stupid she thinks Wu-Tang
is an orange-flavored drink.

Yo' mama's so stupid she ordered
a cheeseburger from McDonald's
and said "Hold the cheese."

I told yo' mama drinks were on the
house...so she went and got a ladder.

Yo' daddy's so dumb it takes him two
hours to watch *60 Minutes*.

Yo' sister is so stupid that when
she missed her period she went to the
Lost and Found.

Yo' sister's so dumb
she searched the store for Dusk liquid
to use for the supper dishes.

Yo' mama's so dumb, when her computer
says, "You've got mail," she runs outside
to look in the mailbox.

LORD BYRON ON WILLIAM SHAKESPEARE

Shakespeare's name, you may depend
on it, stands absurdly high and
will go down. He had no invention
as to stories, none whatever.
He took all his plots from old novels,
and threw their stories into a dramatic
shape, at as little expense of thought
as you or I could turn his plays
back again into prose tales.

Yo' brother's so stupid he planted
Cheerios so he could grow a donut tree.

Your dog's so stupid he buried
his own tail.

Yo' mama so stupid she got locked in a
bathroom and nearly peed her pants.

The worst six years of yo' mama's life
were Grade Three.

Yo' dog is so stupid he chases parked cars.

Yo' daddy's so dumb
he can't pass a urine test.

Yo' mama's like yesterday's coffee—
a little weak in the bean.

Yo' mama's so dumb she tried to put her
M&Ms in alphabetical order.

Yo' mama's so stupid
she got locked in the supermarket
and nearly starved to death.

Yo' daddy's so stupid he has to unzip his pants to count to 11.

Yo' mama is so stupid she thought a hot meal was stolen food!

CHARLES DARWIN ON WILLIAM SHAKESPEARE
I have tried lately to read Shakespeare and found it so intolerably dull that it nauseated me.

In conclusion, just so we're clear on this:

Yo' mama's so dumb…

she's a few clowns short of a circus.

she's a few fries short of a Happy Meal.

she's a few sandwiches short of a picnic.

she's a few beers short of a six-pack.

she's a few peas short of a casserole.

she's an experiment in artificial stupidity.

the wheel's spinning,
but the hamster's dead.

she's a few Rice Krispies shy of a bowl.

the chimney's clogged.

she's as sharp as Jell-O.

she doesn't have all her dogs on a leash.

her elevator doesn't go all the way
to the top floor.

she forgot to pay her brain bill
so it got turned off.

her sewing machine's out of thread.

her antenna doesn't pick up
all the channels.

... she goes to a restaurant, looks at the menu, and says, "I'll take it!"

Yo' mama's so fat you could use her underwear as a parachute.

Yo' mama's so fat, when she backs up she beeps.

Yo' sister's butt is so big she has more crack than a drug dealer.

Yo' mama looks like she was poured into her clothes and forgot to say when.

Yo' mama's so fat every time she turns around it's her birthday.

Yo' mama's so fat, when she steps on the scale it says, "To be continued."

Yo' mama's so fat people exercise by jogging around her!

Yo' mama's so fat she wears an asteroid belt.

Yo' mama's once, twice, three times a lady.

Yo' mama's so fat, when she turns around they throw her a welcome back party.

Yo' mama's so fat she shows up on radar.

Yo' mama's got a new career in the movies—she's the screen.

MUHAMMAD ALI ON JOE FRAZIER
Joe Frazier is so ugly
he should donate his face to
the U.S. Bureau of Wildlife.

Yo' mama once said, "I could eat a horse"…and she did!

Your daddy's so fat he deep-fries
his toothpaste.

Yo' mama's so fat she's half Italian,
half Irish, and half American.

Yo' mama's so fat she fell off a cruise ship
and the captain yelled, "Land Ho!"

Yo' brother's so fat even Richard Simmons
said, "I give up!"

Yo' mama's so fat NASA plans to use her
to plug the hole in the ozone layer.

The only thing that's attracted to yo' mama is gravity.

Yo' mama's so fat you can see her from space.

Yo' mama's so fat her measurements are 36-24-36…and the other arm is just as big.

When you tell yo' mama to haul ass, she's gotta make two trips.

Yo' sister lost at hide-and-seek because I spotted her…behind a sequoia.

Yo' mama's so fat
she could be the eighth continent.

JOE FRAZIER ON MUHAMMAD ALI
He's phony, using his blackness
to get his way.

Yo' mama's so fat
her favorite food is seconds.

Yo' mama's so fat her belt size is "Equator."

Yo' mama's so fat she eats
wide-screen TV dinners.

You were such a fat baby your parents
used a fork lift for a high-chair!

Yo' brother's so fat he needs to put a foot
each on two scales to weigh himself.

ETHEL MERMAN ON COLE PORTER
He sang like a hinge.

Yo' mama's so fat she fell into
the Grand Canyon...and got stuck!

You're so fat you got baptized
at Sea World.

You're so fat you use hula-hoops
to keep your socks up.

Yo' sister's so fat she wears bowling balls
as earrings.

Yo' mama's so fat, on a scale of 1 to 10
she a 747.

Yo' mama's so fat, when she gets a pedicure,
she has to take the girl's word for it.

Yo' mama's so fat, when she went to the
beach, she caused a tsunami.

Yo' daddy's so fat he's got his own
Zip Code.

Yo' mama's so fat she's on BOTH sides
of the family.

Yo' mama's so fat she has more
gravitational pull than a black hole.

Yo' mama's so fat, when she goes
to a restaurant, she even orders the
"Thank You, Come Again."

When you're as fat as yo' mama,
"All you can eat" still ain't enough.

Yo' sister's so fat she eats Wheat Thicks.

MAMIE VAN DOREN ON WARREN BEATTY
**He's the type of man who will
end up dying in his own arms.**

Yo' mama's so fat she lay on the beach and
people ran up and yelled, "Free Willy!"

Yo' daddy's so fat he's got to pull down his
pants to check his pockets.

Yo' mama's so fat, when she bungee jumps,
she brings down the bridge.

Yo' mama's so fat, when she steps on a
scale it reads, "One at a time, please."

Yo' mama's so fat she fell in love
and broke it.

Yo' mama's so fat she looks like she's
smuggling a Volkswagen.

Yo' mama's so fat her thong could diaper
a two-year-old.

Yo' sister's legs are so fat she wears two
skirts instead of pants.

Yo' mama's so fat I had to take a train and
two buses just to get on her good side.

Yo' mama's so fat she wakes up in shifts.

Yo' mama's so fat she sat
on a quarter and snot shot out
of George Washington's nose.

Yo' mama's so fat, when she goes to the
beach no one else gets any sun.

Yo' mama's so fat she can't even
jump to a conclusion.

BOY GEORGE ON PRINCE

**He looks like a dwarf who's been
dipped in a bucket of pubic hair.**

Yo' mama's so fat she's got more chins
than a Hong Kong phone book.

Yo' mama's so fat, when she walks in high
heels, she strikes oil.

Yo' mama's so fat she sat on the beach and
Greenpeace hung a flag on her.

Yo' sister's so fat she went swimming in
the ocean and got harpooned.

Yo' mama's so fat she broke her leg
and gravy poured out.

Yo' mama's so fat you have to grease the
bathtub to get her out.

Yo' daddy's so fat his pinkie ring would be
too big for my thumb.

Yo' mama's so fat she got hit by a bus and said, "Who threw that rock?"

We brought yo' mama to the drive-in and didn't have to pay because we dressed her as a Chevrolet.

Yo' mama's so fat, when she goes to a restaurant, she doesn't get a menu, she gets an estimate.

Yo' mama's so fat she doesn't get tattooed, she gets branded.

Yo' mama's so fat, when she sat on a bus, she made four taxis.

MARK TWAIN ON EDGAR ALLAN POE

His prose is unreadable, like Jane Austen's. No, there is a difference. I could read his prose on a salary, but not Jane's.

Yo' mama's so fat, when she walked in front of the TV, I missed three commercials.

Yo' mama's so fat, when she plays
king of the hill, she's the hill!

Yo' mama's so fat, when she wears
corduroys she smooths out the ridges.

Yo' mama's so fat she sank the *Titanic.*

Yo' mama's so fat, when she jumped
in the ocean, whales started singing
"We Are Family!"

Yo' mama's butt is so big
she got busted in the airport
for having 200 pounds of crack.

Yo' mama's so fat I put a quarter in her
ear and she spat out a bag of Doritos.

Yo' mama's so fat
she rented a stretch limo, sat in the back,
and still crowded the driver.

You're so fat Goodyear wants to fly you
over the Super Bowl.

You're so fat you take up four branches
of your family tree.

Yo' mama's so fat a run in her stocking
leaves her winded.

Yo' mama's so fat she had her portrait
painted with a roller.

WILLIAM FAULKNER ON MARK TWAIN
A hack writer who would not have been
considered fourth rate in Europe,
who tried out a few of the old proven
"sure-fire" literary skeletons with
sufficient local color to intrigue the
superficial and the lazy.

You're so fat your family has to pay
property taxes on you.

You're so fat you could sell shade.

Yo' mama's so fat her belly button's
got an echo.

Yo' mama's so fat she thinks
Barnum & Bailey are clothing designers.

FRIEDRICH NIETZSCHE ON DANTE
A hyena that wrote poetry in tombs.

Yo' mama's so fat that they had to change
"one size fits all" to "one size fits most."

Yo' daddy's so fat he has TB...two bellies.

Yo' mama's so fat somebody wrote "Place Your Ad Here" on each of her butt cheeks.

HERMAN MELVILLE ON RALPH WALDO EMERSON
I could readily see in Emerson a gaping flaw. It was the insinuation that had he lived in those days when the world was made, he might have offered some valuable suggestions.

Yo' brother's so fat after he got off the carousel the horse limped for a week.

Yo' mama's so fat it takes three cows just to make her a pair of shoes.

Yo' mama's so fat her ass has its own congressman.

Yo' mama's so fat her butt looks like two pigs fighting over a milk dud.

Yo' mama's so fat her belly button doesn't have lint, it has sweaters.

Yo' mama's so fat her blood type is Ragu.

Yo' mama's 36-24-36…but that's in feet.

Yo' mama's so fat her cereal bowl
came with a lifeguard.

Yo' mama's so fat her driver's license says,
"Picture continued on other side."

Yo' sister's so fat her favorite blouse
is a maternity dress.

Yo' mama's so fat her picture
needs two frames.

Yo' mama's so fat I gain weight
just *watching* her eat.

CHRISTOPHER PLUMMER ON JULIE ANDREWS
Working with her is like being hit over the head with a Valentine card.

Yo' mama's so fat you gotta take three
steps back just to see all of her.

Yo' mama's so fat, if she weighed five more pounds, she could get group insurance.

Yo' mama's so fat, instead of Levi's 501 jeans, she wears Levi's 1002's.

Yo' mama's so fat her car has to have a sign saying Wide Load.

Yo' mama's so fat Jenny Craig did a credit check.

Yo' mama's so fat last time she went to Sea World, Shamu got turned on.

Yo' mama's so fat she has to call Sherwin-Williams
to paint her toenails.

Yo' mama's so fat her height's the same
whether she's lying down or standing up.

Yo' brother's so fat he can't lose weight,
only find it.

BETTE DAVIS ON JOAN CRAWFORD
The best time I had with Joan Crawford
was when I pushed her down the stairs
in Whatever Happened to Baby Jane?

Yo' mama's so fat she doesn't wear
a G-string, she wears an A, B, C, D, E, F,
and G-string.

HEDDA HOPPER ON JAMES DEAN
Another dirty shirttail
actor from New York.

Yo' mama's so fat she eats cereal
out of a satellite dish.

Yo' mama's so fat she fills up the bathtub,
and then she turns on the water.

Yo' mama's so fat she gets clothes
in three sizes: extra large, jumbo, and
oh-my-god-it's-coming-toward-us!

Yo' mama's so fat she has more nooks and crannies than a Thomas's English Muffin.

Yo' daddy's so fat he has to get out of the car to change gears.

Yo' brother's so fat he has to keep pesos in one pocket and yen in the other.

Yo' mama's so fat she has to put her belt on with a boomerang.

Yo' brother's so fat he uses sleeping bags for tube socks.

Yo' mama's so fat she has two stomachs:
one for meat, one for vegetables.

Yo' sister's so fat she plays hopscotch like
this: LA, Detroit, Seattle, NY.

Yo' mama's so fat she puts mayonnaise
on aspirin.

Yo' mama's so fat she shops for clothes
in the local tent shop.

Yo' mama's so fat she stepped on a scale
and saw her phone number.

———

Yo' mama's so fat she went on a light diet:
as soon as it's light she starts eating.

ELIA KAZAN ON JAMES DEAN
He was a hero to the people who saw
him only as a little waif, when
actually he was a pudding of hatred.

Yo' mama's so fat the body snatchers
called home for backup.

Yo' mama's so fat the horse on her
Polo shirt is real.

Yo' mama's so fat the *shadow* of her ass weighs 50 pounds.

Yo' mama's so fat, when she gets in an elevator, it *has* to go down.

Yo' mama's so fat, when she hauls ass, the National Guard has to help.

Yo' mama's so fat all the restaurants in town have signs that say, "Maximum Occupancy: 240 Patrons OR Yo' Mama."

Yo' daddy's so fat, when he opens the refrigerator, it begs, "Please be gentle."

Yo' sister's so fat, when she ran away they had to use all four sides of the milk carton.

Yo' mama's so fat she walks across the living room and makes the CD skip... at the radio station.

Yo' mama's so fat, when she saw a school bus drive by she yelled, "Hey! Stop that Twinkie."

Yo' mama's so fat, when she was diagnosed with the flesh-eating disease the doctor gave her five years to live.

Yo' mama's so fat, when she sits down she registers 6.0 on the Richter scale.

Yo' mama's so fat, after sex she rolls over and smokes a ham.

JOAN RIVERS ON BO DEREK
She turned down the role of Helen Keller because she couldn't remember the lines.

Yo' mama's so fat, when she takes a shower her feet don't get wet.

Yo' daddy's so fat, when he tiptoes in,
everyone yells, "Stampede!"

FRANK CAPRA ON JOHN FORD
John is a half-tyrant,
half-revolutionary; half-saint,
half-Satan; half-possible,
half-impossible; half-genius,
half-Irish.

Yo' mama's so fat, when she was born,
she didn't get a birth certificate,
she got blueprints.

Yo' mama's so fat, when she travels
she's gotta make two trips.

Yo' mama's so fat, when she walks
in her corduroys you can smell smoke.

Yo' mama's so fat, when she wears a
purple sweater people call her "Barney."

Yo' mama's so fat she uses redwoods
as toothpicks.

Yo' daddy's so fat the National Weather
Service has to assign names to his farts.

Yo' sister's so fat she's been zoned
for commercial development.

Yo' brother's so fat he needs a sock
for each toe.

Yo' mama's so fat, when she wears a yellow
raincoat, kids think she's the school bus.

Yo' mama's so fat she joined an online
dating service and they matched her up
with Detroit.

Yo' mama's so fat she wanted a water bed,
so they put a blanket across Lake Michigan.

Yo' brother's so fat, when he went to the Rose Parade they thought he was a float.

Yo' mama's so fat the police showed her a picture of her feet and she couldn't identify them.

BETTE DAVIS ON JAYNE MANSFIELD
Dramatic art in her opinion is knowing how to fill a sweater.

Yo' mama's so fat on Halloween she says, "Trick or meatloaf!"

Yo' mama's so fat she doesn't have
a doctor, she has a grounds keeper.

ROBERT REDFORD ON PAUL NEWMAN
He has the attention span
of a lightning bolt.

Yo' mama's so fat the elephants at the zoo
throw HER peanuts.

Yo' mama's so fat she's on a new diet plan:
Slim-Slow.

Yo' brother's so fat he freebases salami.

Yo' mama's so fat she wears a three-piece bathing suit.

Yo' mama's so fat she stepped on a talking scale and it told her, "I quit! They don't pay me enough!"

Yo' daddy's so fat he got an EZ Pass for Dairy Queen.

Yo' mama's so fat she makes Big Bird look like a rubber duck.

Yo' brother's so fat his sneakers need license plates.

Yo' mama's butt is so big she bent over and got arrested for selling crack.

Yo' mama's mouth is so big she speaks in Surround Sound.

Yo' brother's so fat he sat on a Nintendo Gamecube and it turned into a Game Boy.

Yo' mama's so fat she farted and launched herself into orbit.

Yo' mama's so fat, when she runs
she sets off car alarms.

TRUMAN CAPOTE ON MERYL STREEP
Oh God! She looks like a chicken.

When God said "Let there be light"
he told yo' mama to move out of the way.

Yo' mama's so fat she sews her clothes
with rope.

I've known yo' sister all my life
and I still haven't seen *all* of her.

Yo' mama's so fat, when she stood in front of the HOLLYWOOD sign it said "H D."

TATUM O'NEAL ON SHIRLEY TEMPLE
She wasn't very good.
She was fine when she was six or seven, but did you notice how she couldn't act when she was fourteen?

Yo' mama's so fat she uses a bath towel as a washcloth.

Yo' mama's so fat she was born with a silver shovel in her mouth.

Yo' mama's so fat she got a run
in her blue jeans.

Yo' daddy's so fat he needs to buy two
airline tickets.

Yo' brother's so fat he fell down and rocked
himself to sleep trying to get up again.

Yo' daddy's so fat the pizza man doesn't
bother to slice the pie for him.

Yo' mama's so fat that when I tried to
drive around her I ran out of gas.

Yo' brother was so fat as a baby, he had dent stripes all around from his crib slats.

Yo' mama's so fat that when she dances she makes the band skip.

Yo' sister's wedding dress was designed by Omar the tent maker.

Yo' mama's so fat she lives in two time zones.

Yo' mama's so fat they had to install speed bumps at the all-u-can-eat buffet.

Yo' mama's so fat you have to grease the door frame and hold a Twinkie on the other side just to get her in the house.

JOHNNY ROTTEN ON BILLY IDOL
The Perry Como of Punk.

Yo' mama's so fat she boarded an airplane and it turned into a submarine.

Yo' mama's so fat she has McDonald's on speed dial.

chapter three
YO' MAMA'S SO UGLY...

... her shadow ran away.

Yo' mama's so ugly she looked out the window and got arrested for mooning.

Yo' sister's so ugly, when she walks into a bank they turn off the surveillance cameras.

If beauty is skin deep, yo' mama's rotten to the core.

Yo' sister's so ugly yo' mama had to be drunk to breastfeed her.

Yo' daddy's so ugly he was the model for Mr. Potato-Head.

Yo' mama's so ugly, when they took her
to the beautician it took 12 hours…
to get a price quote.

Yo' mama's so ugly her mirrors need to be
made of tempered glass.

Yo' mama's so ugly even Rice Krispies
won't talk to her.

Yo' sister's so ugly she turned Medusa
to stone.

Yo' mama's so ugly she makes
Michael Jackson look like Brad Pitt.

CHARLES BARKLEY ON DENNIS RODMAN
Dennis has become like a prostitute
but now it's gotten ridiculous, to the
point where he will do anything
humanly possible to make money.

Minutes after yo' mama was born, her
mama shouted, "What a treasure!" and her
daddy said, "Yeah, now let's go and bury it."

Yo' mama's so ugly yo' daddy takes her
to work every day so he doesn't have to
kiss her good-bye.

Yo' brother's so ugly they knew
the exact time he was born because
his face stopped the clock.

Yo' sister's so ugly she's got marks on her
from people poking her with ten-foot poles.

Yo' sister's so ugly hotel managers
use her picture to keep away the rats.

Yo' brother's so ugly he walked into
the Haunted House and came out
with a job application.

Yo' mama's so ugly she can't go
to the beach because stray cats try
to bury her in the sand.

Yo' mama was so ugly when she was born,
the doctors put her in an incubator with
tinted windows.

Yo' mama's so ugly that when she threw a
boomerang, it refused to come back.

Yo' mama's so ugly her American Express
card left home without her.

Even yo' mama's car is ugly. Somebody
broke into it just to steal the Club.

DAVID BOWIE ON MICK JAGGER
I think Mick Jagger would be
astounded and amazed if he realized
to how many people he is not a
sex symbol but a mother image.

Yo' daddy's so ugly his hairline isn't
receding—his hair is running away
from his face.

Yo' mama's so ugly her psychiatrist makes her lie face down on the couch.

Yo' sister's so ugly Prince Charming would rather live as a frog than kiss her.

JOAN RIVERS ON BOY GEORGE

Boy George is all England needs— another queen who can't dress.

Yo' brother's so ugly he looks better when he shaves his butt and walks backward.

Yo' sister's so ugly that blind men
refuse to have sex with her.

Yo' mama's so ugly she gives Freddy
Kreuger nightmares.

Yo' sister's so ugly for Halloween she
trick-or-treats on the phone!

I heard that you were a ladykiller. They
take one look at you and die of shock.

Sure, I've seen people like you before—
but I had to pay admission.

You're so ugly your dog has to close its eyes when it mounts your leg.

You're so ugly the passport office asked you for a silhouette instead of a photo.

When you were born, the doctor didn't know which end to slap.

I see your sister just came back from the beauty parlor. Apparently it was closed.

Yo' sister's so ugly she gets her hair cut in a pet salon.

Yo' sister looks like a million bucks: all green and wrinkled.

BRITT EKLUND ON ROD STEWART
He was so mean it hurt him to go to the bathroom.

You're so ugly that when you walk into the room the mice scream and jump up on the chairs.

Was anyone else hurt in the accident?

She's so ugly, when I took her
to the zoo, the zookeeper said,
"Thanks for bringing her back!"

Yo' mama's so ugly the Elephant Man
paid to see *her*.

Yo' mama's so ugly,
when she tried to work a street corner,
the johns paid her to leave.

Yo' sister's so ugly she walks down
the street and gets arrested
for attempted murder.

Yo' daddy's so ugly
it looks like his neck threw up.

You mama's so ugly, when she walks by the
bathroom the toilet flushes.

Yo' mama's so ugly, when she joined an ugly
contest they said, "Sorry, no professionals."

Yo' mama's so ugly when she looks in the
mirror the reflection is shaking its head.

Yo' mama's so ugly her birth certificate
came with a letter of apology
from the condom factory.

Yo' mama's so ugly no insect will bite her.

Yo' mama's so ugly she could scare
the flies off a garbage truck.

CHARLES BAUDELAIRE ON RICHARD WAGNER
I love Wagner, but the music I prefer
is that of a cat hung by its tail
outside a window and trying to stick
to the panes of glass with its claws.

I hear you are very kind to animals, so
please give that face back to the gorilla.

Yo' mama's so ugly the last time
I saw something that looked like her,
I pinned a tail on it.

If I were as ugly as you are,
I wouldn't say hello, I'd say boo!

Moonlight becomes you—
total darkness even more.

Yo' daddy's so ugly his electric razor needs
to have four-wheel drive.

Yo' mama's so ugly people go as *her*
for Halloween.

———

Yo' mama's so ugly we put her in the kennel when we go on vacation.

Yo' mama's so ugly people at the circus pay money NOT to see her.

Yo' mama's so ugly, when she moved into her new house all her neighbors chipped in for curtains.

Yo' mama's so ugly she scared the monster out of Loch Ness.

Yo' mama climbed the ugly ladder and didn't miss a rung.

Yo' mama's so ugly your parents met at the zoo.

Yo' mama didn't get hit with the ugly stick, she ran smack into the ugly TREE.

MARTIN SHEEN ON GEORGE W. BUSH
He is like a bad comic working the crowd. A moron, if you'll pardon the expression.

Your sister's so ugly her mama had to tie a steak around her neck to get the dog to play with her.

Yo' mama's so ugly she makes blind children cry.

Yo' mama's so ugly her picture is on the inside of a Roach Motel.

Yo' mama's so ugly people hang her picture in their cars so their radios don't get stolen.

Yo' mama's so ugly she gets seven years' bad luck just for looking at herself in the mirror.

Yo' mama's so ugly she practices birth control by leaving the lights on.

Yo' mama's so ugly her dentist treats her by mail-order.

If ugly were an Olympic event, yo' mama
would be the dream team.

Your sister's so ugly your parents wish
birth control was retroactive.

Yo' mama's so ugly, when she was born
they named her "Damn!"

Yo' sister's so ugly, when she was born the
doctor smacked your parents.

Yo' mama's so ugly, when she was born
the doctor looked at her ass,
then her face, and said, "Twins!"

BILL MAHER ON MICHAEL JACKSON
Fame has sent a number of celebrities off the deep end, and in the case of Michael Jackson, to the kiddie pool.

Yo' mama's so ugly that when she asked for a sex change, the surgeon had to flip a coin.

Yo' mama's so ugly the last time she heard a whistle was when she got hit by a train.

Yo' mama's so ugly she was a guard for Castle Dracula.

If ugly were a crime,
yo' sister would get the electric chair.

Yo' mama's so ugly she scared the stitches
off Frankenstein.

BOY GEORGE ON GEORGE MICHAEL
Sleeping with George Michael would be
like having sex with a groundhog.

Yo' mama's so ugly they pay her
to put her clothes on in strip joints.

Yo' daddy's so ugly, if he was a scarecrow
the corn would run away.

Yo' mama was such an ugly baby
her parents had to feed her with a slingshot.

When I last saw a mouth like yo' sister's,
it had a hook in it.

Whatever kind of look you were aiming
for, you missed.

Yo' father's so ugly they leave his photo
off his Wanted posters.

She's so ugly she'd make a freight train
take a dirt road.

Really, I think yo' mama is a saint...
a Saint Bernard.

Yo' daddy's so ugly he couldn't get laid
in a monkey whorehouse carrying
a bag of bananas.

You're so ugly the dentist needs to take
Novocain to work on you.

I don't have anything bad to say about yo'
mama...her face says it all!

chapter four
YO' MAMA's So oLD...

...Indiana Jones just found cave paintings of her.

Yo' mama's so old, when she was in school there was no history class.

Yo' mama's so old her Social Security number is 1.

Yo' mama's so old her birth certificate expired.

Yo' daddy's so old he drove a chariot to school.

Yo' mama's so old I told her to act her age and she died.

Yo' mama's so old she remembers when the Great Wall of China was just "okay."

Yo' mama's so old she knew Burger King when he was still a prince.

Yo' mama's so old she knew Mr. Clean when he had a comb-over.

Yo' daddy's so old he helped fertilize the Garden of Eden.

Yo' mama knew Madame Butterfly when she was Madame Caterpillar.

When yo' daddy was a kid, the Dead Sea was just coming down with something.

JOAN RIVERS ON YOKO ONO

If I found her floating in my pool, I'd punish my dog.

Yo' mama's so old she remembers when the Grand Canyon was just a ditch.

Yo' mama's so old she was a waitress at the Last Supper.

Yo' mama's so old she left her purse
on Noah's Ark.

Yo' mama's so old *Jurassic Park* brought
back fond memories.

Yo' mama's so old she knew Cap'n Crunch
when he was still a private.

Yo' mama's so old her hot flashes set off
the smoke detectors.

Yo' daddy's so old I asked him for his
business card and he handed me a rock.

Yo' mama's so old Yoda calls her
"young lady."

Yo' mama's so old her first job was
as Cain and Abel's babysitter.

Yo' mama's so old she invented the term
"oldest profession in the world."

Yo' mama's so old that when God said,
"Let there be light," she was the one
flicking the switch.

Yo' mama's so old her birth certificate
is written in Roman numerals.

BETTE MIDLER ON PRINCESS ANNE
Such an active lass.
So outdoorsy. She loves nature
in spite of what it did to her.

Yo' mama's so old her back goes out
more than she does.

Yo' mama's so old she sank her teeth
into a steak and they stayed there.

Yo' daddy's so old he knows everything.
He just can't remember any of it.

Yo' mama is like a used car:
the paint job hides the age until you
study the dents and mileage.

JOAN RIVERS ON MADONNA

She's so hairy, when she lifted up
her arm I thought it was
Tina Turner in her armpit.

Yo' mama says she's pushing 40.
More like dragging it.

When she was 16, the president
gave her a prize for her great beauty.
Hard to believe Calvin Coolidge
had time for such frivolous stuff.

Yo' mama was born in the Chinese Year
of the Brontosaurus.

Yo' mama's so old her memory
is in black and white.

Yo' brother's so old he DJ'd at the
Boston Tea Party.

Yo' mama's so old she took her driver's test on a dinosaur.

Yo' mama's so old her report cards were in hieroglyphics.

SIR JOHN GIELGUD ON INGRID BERGMAN
She speaks five languages and can't act in any of them.

Yo' mama's so old the key on Ben Franklin's kite was to her apartment.

RICHARD BURTON ON ELIZABETH TAYLOR
She has an insipid double chin,
her legs are too short,
and she has a slight potbelly.

Yo' sister's so old she has a vibrator
with a pull-start.

Yo' daddy's so old he farts dust.

Yo' mama's so old she used to braid
Betty Rubble's hair.

Yo' mama's so old she's in Methuselah's yearbook.

I've seen stale raisins with fewer wrinkles than you have!

Yo' mama's so old she has all the apostles in her black book.

Yo' mama's so old she has an autographed Bible.

Yo' mama suffers from Mallzheimer's disease—she goes shopping and forgets where she parked her car.

Yo' mama's so old the candles cost more than the birthday cake.

Yo' mama's so old her breasts secrete powdered milk.

RONALD REAGAN ON

PRIME MINISTER MARGARET THATCHER

The best man in England.

Yo' mama's so old she sat next to Jesus in third grade.

Yo' daddy's so old his blood type
was discontinued.

Yo' mama's so old she helped milk the farm
animals on the Ark.

Yo' mama so old she's still got spots in front
of her eyes from the Big Bang.

AMBROSE BIERCE ON OSCAR WILDE
There never was an impostor
so hateful, a blockhead so stupid, a crank
so variously and offensively daft.
He makes me tired.

HUNTER S. THOMPSON ON HUBERT HUMPHREY
Any political party that can't cough up anything better than a treacherous, brain-damaged old vulture like Hubert Humphrey deserves every beating it gets.

Yo' daddy's so old his wild oats turned to All-Bran with prunes.

Yo' sister's so old she went to an antique auction and three people bid on her.

If yo' mama was a car it would be time to roll back her odometer.

GOLDA MEIR ON MOSHE DAYAN
Don't be so humble, Moshe,
you're not that great.

How can I tell that yo' mama is so old?
Maybe it's the vultures circling the house.

Yo' brother's so old
his sneakers say Air Jesus.

Yo' mama's so old
it looks like the Wrinkle Fairy
tap-danced on her face.

Yo' Mama's so old she still owes Columbus a nickel.

Yo' mama's so old she's like...

an archer: she just bows and quivers.

a banker: she loses interest.

a basketball player:
she stands there and dribbles.

a cleaning lady: time to kick the bucket.

a farmer: she's gone to seed.

a drug dealer: she's gone to pot.

a librarian: she's ready to check out.

a minister: she should be put out to
pastor.

a musician: she's played out.

a pilot: soon she'll be on a higher plane.

a quarterback: she nearly passed away.

a sculptor: she's lost her marbles.

a sewer worker: she's wasting away.

a sailor: she's a little dingy.

a wrestler: she's lost her grip.

Yo' daddy's so old some of his favorite songs are...

"Mrs. Brown You've Got a Lovely Walker"

"You Can't Always Pee When You Want"

"Bad Prune Rising"

"Talkin' 'Bout My Medication"

"You're So Varicose Vein"

"How Can You Mend a Broken Hip?"

"Papa Got a Kidney Stone"

"Denture Queen"

"Once, Twice, Three Trips to the Bathroom"

"A Whiter Shade of Hair"

"With a Little Help from Depends"

Yo' daddy's so old his favorite adult film is *Debby Does Dialysis*.

Yo' daddy's so old, if someone says, "Let's go upstairs and make love," he has to choose one or the other.

JOHNNY CARSON ON CHEVY CHASE

He couldn't ad-lib a fart
after a baked-bean dinner.

You're so old one
of your friends complimented you
on your new alligator shoes—
but you were barefoot at the time.

Yo' brother's so old
they don't give him X-rays anymore—
they just hold him up to the light.

You're so old, when they lit the candles on your birthday cake, a group of campers formed a circle and started singing "Kumbaya."

Yo' brother's so old his definition of "happy hour" is a nap.

Yo' daddy's so old that when a beautiful woman said, "I'm here to give you super sex," he said, "I'll take the soup."

Yo' sister's so old it takes her twice as long to look half as good.

You're so old that the twinkle
in your eye is only the reflection
of the sun on your bifocals.

Yo' daddy's so old he not only remembers
the Alamo but fought at it.

Yo' mama's so old
she's got Jesus' beeper number.

You're so old you sit in a rocking chair
and can't get it going.

Yo' mama's so old, when she sucks in
her gut her ankles swell.

MARLON BRANDO ON MONTGOMERY CLIFT
He acts like he's got a Mixmaster
up his ass and doesn't want anyone
to know it.

Yo' daddy's so old his joints are more
accurate than the National Weather Service.

Yo' brother's so old
the sexy lady he had tattooed on his arm
now looks like yo' mama.

Yo' mama's so old,
when she needs to measure her bustline
she has to measure her waist.

————

Yo' mama's so old
Boy Scouts are standing by to help her
across every street.

Yo' mama was complimented
on her "layered look"…when she was
wearing a bikini.

PHYLLIS DILLER ON MICKEY ROONEY
His favorite exercise
is climbing tall people.

You're so old your blood has faded.

Yo' daddy's so old he Tivo's
The Price Is Right.

Yo' daddy's so old he thinks pudding
is too tough.

Yo' brother's so old it takes him a couple
of tries to get over a speed bump.

Yo' mama's so old she looks both ways
before crossing a room.

Yo' daddy's so old his childhood toys
are in the natural history museum.

Yo' daddy's so old his favorite movies have
been reissued with sound.

Yo' daddy's so old his ears are hairier
than his head.

Yo' mama's so old she got cable
just for the Weather Channel.

Yo' mama's so old that all of the names
in her little black book end in "M.D."

To yo' daddy, "getting a little action"
means he doesn't need to take a laxative.

To yo' mama, "getting lucky" means
finding her car in the parking lot.

To yo' sister, "tying one on" means
fastening her Medic Alert bracelet.

To yo' brother, "pulling an all-nighter"
means not getting up to pee.

You're so old you finally gave up
all your bad habits—and you still
don't feel good.

chapter five
YO' MAMA's SO POOR...

...she has a big hole in the wall she calls "central air."

Yo' mama's so poor she chases after the garbage truck with a shopping list.

Yo' mama's so poor your family eats cereal with a fork to save milk.

Yo' mama's so poor she thinks the Last Supper was when the food stamps ran out.

Yo' mama's so poor her cardboard box was repossessed.

Yo' brother's so poor he watches television on an Etch-A-Sketch.

Yo' family's so poor,
every time the wind blows
your address changes.

Yo' mama's so poor,
when I saw her kicking a can
down the street and asked her what
she was doing, she said, "Moving."

Yo' mama's so poor
she can't afford to pay attention.

I visited yo' mama's house and swiped
away the cobwebs. She screamed, "How
dare you tear down the drapes?!"

JOAN CRAWFORD ON JUDY GARLAND
I didn't know her well,
but after watching her in action
I didn't want to know her well.

Yo' mama's so poor,
when I saw her wobbling down
the street wearing one shoe
I asked, "Lost a shoe?" and she said,
"Nope…found one!"

Yo' mama's so poor she goes to KFC
to lick other people's fingers.

Yo' mama is so poor, I asked what's for dinner and she put her feet on the table and said, "Corn."

Yo' mama's so poor she had to take out a second mortgage on her doorway.

Yo' mama's so poor, I crushed out a cigarette burning in her living room ashtray and she shouted, "Hey, who turned off the heater!?"

When yo' mama asked me over to dinner, I took a paper plate from the kitchen and she growled: "Don't use the good china!"

You're so poor panhandlers give you money.

Yo' mama's so poor she bounces
food stamps.

Yo' mama's so poor, when I asked her
what was for dinner she took off her
shoelaces and said, "Spaghetti."

Yo' mama's so poor she got married just
so she could get some rice.

Yo' mama's so poor she can't afford to put
her two cents in.

Yo' mama's so poor I asked to use her bathroom and she handed me two large sticks, one to hold up the ceiling, the other to fight off the cockroaches.

FORMER UK PRIME MINISTER

EDWARD HEATH ON THE BEATLES

Their lyrics are unrecognizable as the Queen's English.

Yo' mama's so poor, she went to K-Mart to buy luggage and came home with a box of Hefty bags.

Yo' mama's so poor, when I pressed her doorbell she leaned out the window and yelled, "DING-DONG!"

KEITH RICHARDS ON SIR ELTON JOHN

His writing is limited
to songs for dead blondes.

Yo' mama's so poor she has to wear her Denny's uniform to church.

When I asked yo' mama what was for dinner she pulled out a gun and said, "Next thing that moves!"

Yo' mama's so poor, when I saw her carrying a carton down the street and asked her what she was doing, she said, "Ain't you ever seen a mobile home?"

Yo' mama's so poor I saw her wrestling a squirrel for a peanut.

Yo' daddy's so poor his favorite dish is road kill.

Yo' mama's so poor, when I walked into her house, two roaches tripped me and a rat stole my wallet.

Yo' mama's so poor I came over for dinner
and she read me some recipes.

Yo' mama's so poor
she has to take the trash *in*.

Yo' brother's so poor
I walked through his front door
and ended up in his backyard.

Yo' mama's so poor her doormat doesn't
say "Welcome," it says "Welfare."

Yo' daddy's so poor his TV has two
channels: ON and OFF.

SIR ELTON JOHN ON KEITH RICHARDS

It would be awful to be like Keith Richards. He's pathetic. It's like a monkey with arthritis trying to go on stage and look young. I have great respect for the Stones but they would have been better if they'd thrown Keith out fifteen years ago.

Yo' mama's so poor she waves around a Popsicle and calls it air-conditioning.

Yo' mama's so poor TV dinner trays are her good china.

Your family's so poor when you want
to watch TV you all go to Sears.

Yo' mama's so poor she puts free samples
on layaway.

Yo' family's so poor they send the cat out
to fetch dinner.

Yo' sister's so poor even the Republicans
are willing to give her welfare.

Yo' brother's so poor burglars break into
his house and *leave* money.

chapter six
She's the Worst:
A Miscellany of Insults

Yo' Mama has a glass eye with a fish in it.

Yo' mama's so nasty she brings crabs
to the beach.

Yo' mama smells so bad
Secret told on her.

Yo' sister's so greasy her freckles slipped off.

Yo' mama's so hairy she shaves
with a Weed Whacker.

Yo' mama's so skinny she has to wear
a belt with her spandex.

Yo' brother's so short, when he's on the
bed he calls it the top bunk.

Yo' daddy's head is so wrinkled
he has to screw his hat on.

You're so bony your knees knock
when they don't even touch.

Yo' mama's so hairy
Bigfoot took a picture of her.

Yo' daddy's so short his backpack
comes with kneepads.

Yo' mama's so skinny she can see through
a peephole with both eyes.

HAROLD ROBBINS ON ERNEST HEMINGWAY
Hemingway was a jerk.

One of yo' mama's legs is so much shorter
than the other that she walks in circles.

Yo' daddy's so smelly female dogs howl
from miles away whenever he scratches.

Yo' mama's so hairy she shaves her tongue!

You're so skinny you have to stand in the
same place twice to cast a shadow.

Yo' mama's so short she can sit on a dime
and swing her legs.

Yo' mama's so hairy every time
she steps outside someone yells,
"RUN, it's King Kong!"

You're so skinny you have to run around
in the shower to get wet.

Yo' daddy's nose is so hairy people think
he has a mustache.

Yo' daddy's so short
he wears your baby clothes
as hand-me-downs.

Yo' mama's so hairy her beautician
shampoos and sets her beard.

Yo' sister's so skinny
she swallowed a meatball and
thought she was pregnant.

Yo' daddy's so smelly he had to file
an injunction with the sanitation
department not to pick him up.

Yo' mama's so nasty the Ivory soap sinks
after she uses it.

LYNDON BAINES JOHNSON ON GERALD FORD
He's a nice guy, but he played too much
football with his helmet off.

Yo' brother's so bucktoothed
he can stick out his tongue without
having to open his mouth.

Yo' daddy's so short, whenever
he goes out to eat waiters offer him
a booster seat.

Yo' mama's so smelly she's her own
bug repellent.

Your glasses are so thick you can see into
the future.

Yo' mama's so nasty a skunk smelled her
and fainted.

Yo' sister's mouth is so big it takes her an
hour to put on her lipstick!

Yo' sister's head is so big, what everyone
thinks is an Afro is really a crew cut.

Yo' mama's house is so dirty the cats
ask to go outside instead of using
their litter box.

Yo' brother's breath is so bad his teeth
have to duck when he exhales.

Yo' mama's so hairy she looks like
a Chia Pet with a sweater on.

You're so short you can play racquetball
against the curb.

Yo' mama's so skinny she uses Chapstick
for deodorant.

Yo' mama's so nasty she has to sneak up
on bathwater.

HARRY S TRUMAN ON RICHARD M. NIXON

He is a shifty-eyed goddamn liar.... He's
one of the few in the history of this
country to run for high office talking
out of both sides of his mouth at the
same time and lying out of both sides.

Yo' daddy's so short he tried to commit
suicide with a thumbtack.

Yo' mama's so hairy she went to a hair salon for a trim, then opened up her blouse.

Yo' mama's teeth are so yellow, when she smiles cars slow down.

Yo' brother's breath is so bad you have to use deodorant to wash his dishes.

Yo' mama's so hairy, when she went to the pound to get a dog, the staff tried to put her in a cage.

Yo' mama's house is so dirty I gotta wipe my feet before I go back outside.

Yo' brother's so short, he uses a dog bed as a futon.

Yo' mama's so skinny she cuts up egg cartons to make her own bras.

Yo' sister's so dirty she lost six pounds after taking a shower.

Yo' mama's so hairy, when she got waxed she lost 20 pounds.

Yo' sister's so nasty flies prefer vinegar.

Yo' mama has so many varicose veins
she could double as a road map!

Yo' mama has so many teeth missing, it
looks like her tongue is in jail.

Yo' sister's so skinny she turned sideways
and disappeared.

Yo' mama's so smelly the government
makes her wear a Biohazard warning.

Yo' mama's so nasty ANY e-mail message
from her carries a virus.

Yo' daddy's so short his ladder had to be a
special order with extra rungs.

Yo' daddy's so hairy he goes to a vet
for his flu shots.

Yo' mama's breath is so foul, I don't know
whether to give her gum or toilet paper.

Yo' mama's so nasty she made
Right Guard turn left.

Yo' sister's teeth are so yellow, when she smiles people try to butter them.

GORE VIDAL ON RONALD REAGAN
A triumph of the embalmer's art.

Yo' daddy's so short he still has to show ID at the movies.

Yo' sister's so greasy she uses Lava soap as a beauty bar.

Yo' mama's such a bad cook even the cockroaches won't eat it.

You're so lazy you need to wear an alarm
watch to remind you to use the bathroom.

THOMAS PAINE ON JOHN ADAMS
It has been the political career of this man
to begin with hypocrisy, proceed with
arrogance, and finish with contempt.

Yo' brother's so greasy he fries
in direct sunlight.

You're so slow you raced a pregnant woman
and came in third!

You're so short, when it rains,
you're the last to know!

Yo' mama's glasses are so thick, when she
looks at a map she can see people waving.

Yo' daddy's teeth are so bad he has to use
baby lotion instead of mouthwash.

Yo' mama's arms are so short she has to
tilt her head to scratch her ear.

Yo' mama's so skinny the doctor kept
giving her the rabbit test right into her
ninth month.

———

Yo' brother's so short he needs
a stepstool to get onto his roller skates.

Yo' daddy's so hairy the cat coughs up
furballs every time she licks him.

ROBERT LOUIS STEVENSON ON WALT WHITMAN
A large shaggy dog unchained,
scouring the beaches of the world
and baying at the moon.

Yo' mama's so greasy she sweats butter.

Yo' mama's so skinny you could blindfold
her with dental floss.

Yo' mama's house is so dirty
newcomers can find the bathroom
by smell…once they stop
confusing it with the kitchen.

Yo' daddy's head is so big, when he ties
his shoes, he flips over.

Yo' daddy's so lazy
he orders his burgers well chewed.

You're so skinny
even your shadow can't find you.

Yo' brother's so slow he needs to be
dropped off at school the night before.

Yo' mama's eyes are so crossed tears roll
down her back when she cries.

Yo' mama's so smelly farmers use her
bathwater as liquid fertilizer.

Yo' daddy's so skinny, he keeps his pajama
bottoms up with a shoelace.

Yo' sister's so hairy,
when she puts on a bikini she looks
like she's wearing a belted fur coat.

MARTIN LUTHER ON HENRY VIII

A pig, an ass, a dunghill, the spawn
of an adder, a basilisk, a lying buffoon,
a mad fool with a frothy mouth.

Yo' daddy's so short,
when he drives he needs to be strapped
into a kiddie seat first.

Yo' mama's so skinny
she can hula-hoop with a Cheerio.

You're so bucktoothed
you can eat corn-on-the-cob
through a picket fence.

HERMAN MELVILLE ON RALPH WALDO EMERSON
I could readily see in Emerson
a gaping flaw. It was the insinuation
that had he lived in those days when the
world was made, he might have offered
some valuable suggestions.

Yo' mama's so nasty she bit the dog
and gave it rabies.

Yo' daddy's nose is so big
his middle name is Pinocchio.

You're so greasy yo' mama has to
wring out your sheets before she
puts them in the washer.

Yo' sister's so skinny her toothbrush
only has one row.

Yo' mama's so hairy, fat, and old people
mistake her for Santa Claus.

What's Yo' Mama Like?

Yo' mama is like a gumball machine:
for a nickel, everyone gets a piece!

Yo' mama is like potato chips: Free to Lay!

Yo' mama is like a screen door, after a
couple bangs she tends to loosen up!

Yo' mama is like the Pillsbury Doughboy—
everyone gets a poke!

Yo' mama is like a doorknob:
everyone gets a turn!

Yo' mama is like a bus:
fifty cents and she's good for a ride!

Yo' mama is like a golf course:
everyone gets a hole in one!

Yo' mama is like a hardware store:
four cents a screw!

Yo' mama is like Domino's pizza:
something for nothing.

Yo' mama is like Chinese food:
sweet, sour, and cheap!

Yo' mama is like a birthday cake:
everybody gets a piece.

Yo' mama is like 7-Eleven:
open all night, hot to go, and for 89 cents
you can get a slurpy.

Yo' mama is like Humpty Dumpty: first she
gets humped, then she gets dumped.

Yo' mama is like a bus:
she's big, she doesn't smell very good,
and it's only a dollar to ride her.

Yo' mama is like a nickel:
she ain't worth a dime.

Yo' mama is like a library:
open to the public.

Yo' mama is like a basketball hoop:
everybody gets a shot.

Yo' mama is like a microwave:
one button and she's hot.

Yo' mama is like a street lamp:
she gets turned on every night and hangs
on street corners.

Yo' mama is like a carpenter's dream:
flat as a board and easy to nail.

Yo' mama is like a gas station:
you gotta pay before you pump.

Yo' mama is like a postage stamp:
you lick her, stick her, then send her away.

Yo' mama is like a dollar bill:
she gets handled all across the country.

Yo' mama is like a five-foot-tall basketball
hoop: it ain't that hard to score.

Yo' mama is like McDonald's:
Billions and billions served.

Yo' mama is like a package of batteries:
Ever Ready!

Yo' mama is like an aircraft carrier:
flat top, big bottom, cruises up and down
the coast, and picks up 100 sailors
in every port.

Yo' mama is like Sprint: 10 cents a minute
anywhere in the country.

Yo' mama's like a fast food restaurant—
quick and easy!!!

The difference between yo' mama and a
747? Not everyone has been on a 747.

Insults, Courtesy of William Shakespeare

Here's your chance to sound classy
when you're telling someone to screw off:
a generous selection of comebacks
courtesy of the Bard himself.

Let's meet as little as we can.
—*As You Like It*

He is deformed, crooked, old and sere,
Ill faced, worse bodied,
shapeless and everywhere;
Vicious, ungentle, foolish, blunt, unkind;
Stigmatical in making, worse in mind.
—*The Comedy of Errors*

More of your conversation would infect my
brain. —*Coriolanus*

Away! Thou art poison to my blood.
—*Cymbeline*

Thou damned and luxurious mountain goat.
—*Henry V*

You blocks, you stones, you worse
than senseless things. —*Julius Caesar*

Thou art a boil,
A plague-sore, an embossed carbuncle
In my corrupted blood. —*King Lear*

Beg that thou may have leave to hang
thyself. —*The Merchant of Venice*

Vile worm, thou wast o'erlook'd even in
thy birth. —*The Merry Wives of Windsor*

Tempt not too much
the hatred of my spirit;
For I am sick when I do look on thee.
—*A Midsummer Night's Dream*

Heaven truly knows that thou
are as false as hell. —*Othello*

Thou lump of foul deformity. —*Richard III*

Thou detestable maw, thou womb
of death. —*Romeo and Juliet*

Away, you three-inch fool.
—*The Taming of the Shrew*

Would thou wert clean enough to spit
upon! —*Timon of Athens*

Thou sodden-witted lord!
Thou has no more brain
than I have in mine elbows.
—*Troilus and Cressida*

If you spend word for word with me,
I shall make your wit bankrupt.
—*The Two Gentlemen of Verona*

Go rot!
—*The Winter's Tale*

Chapter Seven
Oh Yeah? Comebacks for Yo' Mama

The jerk store called.
They're running out of you.
—JERRY SEINFELD

I'm going to memorize your name
and then throw my head away.
—OSCAR LEVANT

Like I said—I LOVE yo' Mama. I'm not going to leave her high and dry, all alone to defend herself. Here are some snappy comebacks she can use when the fur starts to fly. It's the least I could do.

100,000 sperm to choose from,
and you were the fastest?

After meeting you, I've decided I am in
favor of abortion in cases of incest.

All that you are, you owe to your parents.
Why don't you send them a penny
and square the account?

You should sue the person who told you
to "just be yourself."

Before you came along we were hungry.
Now we are fed up.

Do you ever wonder what life would be like if you'd had enough oxygen at birth?

BARBARA STANWYCK ON MARILYN MONROE
Her body has gone to her head.

Do you have to leave so soon?
I was about to poison the tea.

You don't know the meaning of the word
"fear"—but then again you don't know the
meaning of most words.

People say I have no taste, but I like you.

I like your approach.
Now let's see your departure.

I may be fat, but you're ugly—
and I can diet.

DON RICKLES ON FRANK SINATRA
When you enter a room, you have to
kiss his ring. I don't mind, but he has it
in his back pocket.

I never forget a face…but in your case
I'll make an exception!

I reprimanded my son for mimicking you.
I told him not to act like a fool.

I understand you, but thousands wouldn't!

I used to think that you were a big pain
in the neck. Now I have a much lower
opinion of you.

Don't feel bad.
A lot of people have no talent!

Don't mind him. He has a soft heart
and a head to match.

Don't you love nature,
despite what it did to you?

Every girl has the right to be ugly,
but you abused the privilege.

Everyone is gifted—but some people
open the package sooner.

This would be an excellent time
to become a missing person.

Folks clap when they see you—
their hands over their eyes.

You've reached rock bottom
and are starting to dig.

Have you considered suing your brains
for nonsupport?

GORE VIDAL ON ANDY WARHOL
The only genius with an IQ of 60.

You could open your mail with that nose!

I wonder if you can think
without moving your lips?

Yo' daddy comes from a long line of real estate people—they're a vacant lot.

Yo' brother does the work of three men: Larry, Curly, and Moe.

AUGUST RENOIR ON LEONARDO DA VINCI

He bores me. He ought to have stuck to his flying machines.

You don't know whether to scratch your watch or wind your butt.

You have depth, but only on the surface.
Down deep inside, you're shallow.

You're dark and handsome.
When it's dark, you're handsome.

Yo' granddaddy left his body to science,
and science is contesting the will.

Is he conceited? He walks down Lover's
Lane holding his own hand.

Yo' daddy would steal the straw
from his mother's kennel.

See, now this is what happens when
cousins marry.

As an outsider,
what do you think of the human race?

You're about as useful as rubber lips
on a woodpecker.

At least you are not obnoxious
like so many other people—you are
obnoxious in your very own way!

Here's 20 cents. Call all your friends
and bring back the change!

You've got that faraway look. The farther
away you get, the better you look.

KEITH RICHARDS ON CHUCK BERRY
I love his work but I couldn't
warm to him even if I was
cremated next to him.

You're so dense that light
bends around you.

You realize you're the first in yo' daddy's
family born without a tail.

Yo' brother's the only man who,
if told to screw himself, could do it.

Hey, I remember you when you had
only one stomach.

Hi! I'm a human being…and yourself?

When yo' daddy was in the military, his
men would follow him anywhere, but only
out of morbid curiosity.

Yo' granddaddy's origins are so low, you'd
have to limbo under his family tree.

Yo' sister's personality's split so many ways
she goes to group therapy alone.

How did you get here?
Did someone leave your cage open?

I bet your mother has a loud bark!

I can tell you are lying.
Your lips are moving.

I can't seem to remember your name...
please don't help me!

I can't talk to you right now; where will
you be in ten years?

I certainly hope you are sterile.

DON RICKLES TO DAVID LETTERMAN
Who picks your clothes—
Stevie Wonder?

I could make a monkey out of you,
but why should I take all the credit?

I don't consider you a vulture.
More like something a vulture would eat.

I don't know what your problem is,
but I'll bet it's hard to pronounce.

I don't mind that you are talking so long
if you don't mind that I'm not listening.

I don't want you to turn the other
cheek—it's just as ugly.

I hear the only place you're ever invited
is outside.

I hear what you're saying
but I just don't care.

I hear you were born on a farm.
How many in the litter?

I hear you were born on April 2;
a day too late!

I hear that you changed your mind.
So, what did you do with the diaper?

I know you are nobody's fool but maybe
someone will adopt you.

I know you're a self-made man.
It's nice of you to take the blame!

I will defend to your death
my right to my opinion.

WOODROW WILSON ON CHESTER A. ARTHUR
A nonentity with side whiskers.

I worship the ground that awaits you.

I would ask you how old you are
but I know you can't count that high.

I would like to insult you, but with your
intelligence you wouldn't get offended.

I would like the pleasure
of your company—but there's
no pleasure in it at all.

PRINCE ON MICHAEL JACKSON
Michael Jackson's album was only called "Bad" because there wasn't enough room on the sleeve for "Pathetic."

I'd hate to see you go,
but I'd love to watch you leave!

I'd like to give you a going-away
present…but you have to do your part.

I'd like to have the spitting concession at
your grave.

I'd like to help you out.
Which way did you come in?

I'd rather pass a kidney stone
than another night with you.

If I promise to miss you, will you go away?

If I said anything to you that I should be
sorry for, I'm glad.

If I throw you a stick, will you leave?

If idiots could fly, this would be an airport.

If ignorance is bliss, you must be orgasmic.

If manure were music,
you'd be a brass band.

If sex were fast food,
you'd have an arch over your head.

If yo' sister was cast as Lady Godiva
the horse would steal the show.

If truth is stranger than fiction,
you must be truth!

If we were to kill everybody
who hates you, it wouldn't be murder;
it would be genocide!

If what you don't know can't hurt you,
you must be practically invulnerable.

If you act like an ass, don't get insulted
if people ride you.

I'll never forget the first time we met—
though I'll keep trying.

I'm busy now. Can
I ignore you some other time?

I'm glad to see you're not letting your
education get in the way of your ignorance.

I'm trying to imagine you with a personality.

In the land of the witless,
the half-wit is king.

Instead of being born again,
why don't you just grow up?

Is that your nose
or are you eating a banana?

It is mind over matter.
I don't mind, because you don't matter.

CHARLIE SHEEN ON COLIN FARRELL
I've got three words for him:
Am. A. Teur.

It's hard to get the big picture
when you have such a small screen.

I've come across decomposed bodies
that are less offensive than you are.

Sometimes love turns out to be
mere infatuation, but the hate I feel
for you is the real thing.

I've seen people like you,
but I had to pay admission!

Keep talking.
I always yawn when I'm interested.

Learn from your parents' mistakes:
use birth control!

Let's play horse.
I'll be the front end and you be yourself.

Make somebody happy.
Mind your own business.

Nice perfume. Must you marinate in it?

Of all the people I've met
you're certainly one of them.

People can't say that you have absolutely
nothing! After all, you have inferiority!

People say that you are outspoken
but not by anyone that I know of.

Perhaps your purpose in life
is to serve as a warning to others.

Please breathe the other way,
you're bleaching my hair.

So, a thought crossed your mind?
Must have been a long and lonely journey.

Some drink from the fountain of
knowledge, but you just gargled.

Some people are has-beens.
You are a never-was.

Someday you'll go far,
if you catch the right train.

Sure, I'd love to help you out...
Which way did you come in?

Take a vacation; go to Club Dead.

That's a very meaty question and I'd like to
give it a very meaty answer: baloney!

The cream rises to the top.
So does the scum.

The more I think of you,
the less I think of you.

EL GRECO ON MICHELANGELO

He was a good man, but he did not
know how to paint.

The next time you shave, could you stand
a little closer to the razor?

The overwhelming power of the sex drive
is clear in the fact that someone was
willing to father you.

The wheel is still spinning
but the hamster died.

The thing that terrifies me most
is that someone might hate me
as much as I loathe you.

Oh, now I see it—
the twinkle in your eyes is actually
the sun shining between your ears.

There are only two things I dislike about
you: your face.

We all spring from apes
but you didn't spring far enough.

We do not complain about your
shortcomings but about your long stayings.

I'll see you in my dreams…
if I eat too much.

When you ran away we put an ad in the paper saying, "Do not come home and all will be forgiven."

We know you could not live without us. We'll pay for the funeral.

What color is the sky on YOUR planet?

Whatever is eating you... must be suffering horribly.

When you feel terrific, notify your face.

When you die, I'd like to go to your funeral but I'll probably have to go to work that day. I believe in business before pleasure.

When you were a child we wanted to hire someone to take care of you— but the Mafia wanted too much.

When you were born God finally admitted that even He makes mistakes!

Which sexual position produces the ugliest children? Ask your mom!

Why don't you slip into something more
comfortable...like a coma.

Would you like to replace my business
partner who died this morning?
I'll arrange it with the undertaker.

You always have your ear to the ground.
So how's life in the gutter?

You are a man of the world, which
explains what sad shape the world is in.

You are down to earth—
but not quite far down enough.

EDGAR DEGAS ON CLAUDE MONET
A skillful but short-lived decorator.

You are no longer beneath my contempt.

You're not as bad as people say...
you're WORSE.

You are pretty as a picture—
and we'd love to hang you.

Are you always this obnoxious or are you
just trying to be nice to me?

———————

You are so boring
you can't even entertain a doubt.

You are so dishonest that I don't even
believe you when you say you are lying!

You are such a smart-ass I bet you
could sit on a carton of ice cream and
tell what flavor it is.

You grow on people—like a wart!

You have a lot of well-wishers. They would
all like to throw you down one.

FRANK SINATRA ON ROBERT REDFORD
Well, at least he has finally
found his true love...
What a pity he can't marry himself.

You have a speech impediment...
your foot.

You have an inferiority complex—
and it's fully justified.

You must have a low opinion of people
if you think they're your equals.

You must have gotten up on the wrong
side of the cage this morning.

You remind me of the ocean—
you make me sick.

You should do some soul-searching.
Maybe you'll find one.

You started at the bottom
and it's been downhill ever since.

You used to be arrogant and obnoxious
but now you're just the opposite:
obnoxious and arrogant.

You will never be able to live down
to your reputation.

You're better at sex than anyone I know.
Now, all you need is a partner.

Did you eat paint chips
when you were a kid?

HOWARD HUGHES ON CLARK GABLE
His ears made him look like a taxicab
with both doors open.

Converse with any plankton lately?

Your mouth is getting too big
for your muzzle.

You're about as useful
as a Betamax video recorder.

You're acquitting yourself in a way
that no jury ever would.

Somebody called you an "idiot savant."
I said, "You're half right."

You're nobody's fool. Let's see if we can
get someone to adopt you.

You're not yourself today.
I noticed the improvement immediately.

There are several people
in this world that I find obnoxious
and you are all of them.

They said you were a great asset.
I told them they were off by two letters.

You're so small you pose for trophies.

BOB COSTAS ON DENNIS RODMAN

He has so many fish hooks in his nose,
he looks like a piece of bait.

They say opposites attract.
I hope you meet someone who is good-
looking, intelligent, and cultured.

They say space is a dangerous place...
especially when it's between your ears!

They say that travel is broadening.
You must have been around the world.

They say that two heads
are better than one. In your case, one
would have been better than none.

You're the best at all you do...
and all you do is make people hate you.

Don't thank me for insulting you.
It was my pleasure.

I Promise I'll Never Use This Book Again

He has a right to criticize who has a heart to help.
—ABRAHAM LINCOLN

Repeat after me: "Okay, Mama, I'm sorry. I know I've been rude, sarcastic, and disrespectful at your expense. I promise I'll shape up and show you the love. I'll never speak unkindly about your weight, your intelligence, your hygiene, your age, or your bank account. And that goes double for Daddy, Sister, and the rest of the family. If it helps, I'll never use this book again. In fact I'll throw it out the window RIGHT NOW. There, I did it. See? It landed in that mud puddle next to the garage. So we're cool, right? MAMA??"

When all else fails, apologize. It doesn't cost you anything, rot your teeth, or give you indigestion—and it'll make yo' mama feel a whole lot better. Otherwise, she just might hit you so hard your next door neighbors will fall down!

The truth is, I hope you enjoy this book for a long time, and use it in the spirit of harmless fun (or constructive criticism). I'm sure the people you hang out with can take a joke or two…or a few hundred. And if you come up with some great insults you'd like to share in a future edition, please e-mail them to me at InsultsJokes@aol.com. I can never get my fill of "yo' mama." Well, you know what I mean.

—Hugh Payne